The FLIGHT of the WILD GANDER

A SKELETON KEY STUDY GUIDE

The FLIGHT *of the* WILD GANDER

A SKELETON KEY STUDY GUIDE

by

EVANS LANSING SMITH, PhD

Copyright © 2023 Joseph Campbell Foundation

All rights reserved. No part of this publication may be reproduced, distributed, or transmitted in any form or by any means, including photocopying, recording, or other electronic or mechanical methods, without the prior written permission of the publisher, except in the case of brief quotations embodied in critical reviews and certain other noncommercial uses permitted by copyright law. For permission requests, please contact the Joseph Campbell Foundation's Rights and Permissions Manager at rights@jcf.org.

ISBN: 978-1-61178-040-6

Front cover image detail from Kṛṣṇa hiding the cows of Brahma, a scene from the Bhaghavata Purana. Guler miniature, eighteenth century. National Museum, New Delhi, India.

Book design by *the*BookDesigners.

First printing edition 2023

www.jcf.org

Contents

About *The Collected Works of Joseph Campbell* and the Joseph Campbell Foundation Skeleton Key Study Guide Series 1

How to Use This Study Guide 3

Skeleton Key Study Guide Introduction
by Evans Lansing Smith, PhD 5

Introduction. 11

CHAPTER I
The Fairy Tale. 19

CHAPTER II
Bios and Mythos. 37

CHAPTER III
Primitive Man as Metaphysician 49

CHAPTER IV
Mythogenesis. 65

CHAPTER V
The Symbol Without Meaning. 81

CHAPTER VI
The Secularization of the Sacred................ 103

Final Thoughts from Evans Lansing Smith, PhD........ 121

About Joseph Campbell.......................... 123

About the Author............................... 125

About the Joseph Campbell Foundation 126

About
The Collected Works of Joseph Campbell
AND THE JOSEPH CAMPBELL FOUNDATION
SKELETON KEY STUDY GUIDE SERIES

At his death in 1987, Joseph Campbell left a significant body of published work that explored his lifelong passion for myths and symbols from many cultures. He also left a large volume of unreleased work: uncollected articles, notes, letters, and diaries, as well as audio- and videotape recorded lectures.

The Joseph Campbell Foundation was founded in 1991 to preserve, promote, and perpetuate Campbell's work. The Foundation has undertaken to archive his papers and recordings in digital format, and to publish previously unavailable material and out-of-print works as *The Collected Works of Joseph Campbell*.

The Foundation is now also publishing this series of Skeleton Key Study Guides to accompany selected titles in the *Collected Works*. We intend study guides such as this one to provide entry points into Campbell's ideas for students and for others new to Campbell studies. We hope that Campbell's work and his way of working inspire you to bring new creativity, mythic awareness, and psychological depth to your own work, as they have already done for so many.

How to Use This Study Guide

A skeleton key can open many locks because it has been filed down to only the essentials. This study guide opens *The Flight of the Wild Gander* the same way. Each chapter of the study guide focuses on a corresponding chapter in *The Flight of the Wild Gander*. In each chapter, you'll find a summary of the *Gander* chapter, section by section, followed by points of interest in that chapter as well as complementary reading and audio lists. Chapters close with a selection of discussion and essay questions, and prompts for creative projects. Our vision is that this Skeleton Key Study Guide unlocks *The Flight of the Wild Gander* for you, whether you are new to the material or deepening your relationship with it.

CITATIONS FROM *THE FLIGHT OF THE WILD GANDER*

Whenever this Skeleton Key Study Guide quotes directly from *The Flight of the Wild Gander*, the text includes footnotes that contain page numbers on which you can find the original citation. These page numbers refer to the edition first printed in June 2002 as part of *The Collected Works of Joseph Campbell*.

Campbell, Joseph. *The Flight of the Wild Gander: Explorations in the Mythological Dimension. The Collected Works of Joseph Campbell.* New World Library, 2002.

Skeleton Key Study Guide Introduction

BY EVANS LANSING SMITH, PhD

"Joy to him whom a noble spirit has encountered in early youth!"[1]

I discovered Joseph Campbell's books at a critical time in my life. I was twenty-six years old. I had just crossed the Irish Sea on a ferry from Wales to Dublin to begin a two-year program in creative writing. That night, I had a powerful archetypal dream, laden with mythological symbolism, which I incorporated into a poem called "Die Lorelei." After I shared the dream with one of my classmates, she said she had a book for me to read—and she lent me her copy of *The Hero with a Thousand Faces*. It was a revelation, and set me on my lifelong journey of studies in comparative literature. By the end of the two years devoted to writing a novel about a young poet writing a novel, I had finished Campbell's epic tome, *Creative Mythology*, which introduced me to the medieval world of the Grail Romances and connected them to my primary interest in the writings of James Joyce and Thomas Mann. When it came time to return home to Baltimore, I wasn't ready, feeling instead eager to pursue the new worlds of European culture Campbell had opened up to me. So when my friend gave me a brochure announcing a study tour of northern France, focusing on the Grail legends and the Middle Ages and led by Joseph Campbell, I signed up immediately.

Full of anticipation, I crossed the English Channel to meet the group at the Charles de Gaulle airport and climbed on the bus for the journey. The next thing I knew, I was sitting with Joseph Campbell, who had been twenty-six years old himself when he first came to Paris to study the Romances of Chrétien de Troyes and Wolfram von Eschenbach. I can't fully communicate the joy of his presence, nor the impact of his inspiring lectures. It was like getting the education I had never had, a real postgraduate seminar. I sat for hours absorbing so much information, brought powerfully to life by Campbell's talent as a storyteller and educator. And I continued to attend his lectures in the years that followed, first in New York at his Theater of the Open Eye—where I saw his wife Jean Erdman's last performance in the role of Anna Livia Plurabelle in *The Coach with Six Insides*— and then in Santa Barbara at week-long seminars at Casa Maria, and again in San Francisco in the early 1980s, for a week of study focused on James Joyce and Thomas Mann, sponsored by the C.G. Jung Institute.

Although I have had the supreme good fortune of studying with truly gifted educators, none had the erudition and genius Campbell had. When he spoke about a subject, he didn't just supply the information needed to understand it; he gave you a direct experience of the material, as if by magic. It has been my great delight to incorporate that material into my many books and articles on the mythology of the underworld in Modernist literature, art, and film, and it has been my goal as a teacher to transmit the powerful inspiration of Campbell's presence, in order to bring the classroom alive. With the encyclopedic intensity of his writings and lectures, that has been a challenge. So it was with joy that I learned that *The Flight of the Wild Gander* had been reissued by New World Library and the Joseph Campbell Foundation in *The Collected Works of Joseph Campbell* series. I have found it to be of inestimable value in my classes, for it serves as an overture to the grand opera of his work.

Skeleton Key Study Guide Introduction

When Joseph Campbell published *The Flight of the Wild Gander* in 1951, he was forty-seven years old. He would continue writing, prolifically, until his death in October of 1987—another thirty-six years. The first volume of his magnum opus, *The Historical Atlas of World Mythology: The Way of the Animal Powers*, came out in 1983. The three parts of the second volume, *The Way of the Seeded Earth*, were published posthumously, from 1988 to 1989. That situates *The Flight of the Wild Gander* approximately in the middle of an extraordinary career, which officially began, you might say, in 1943 when he collaborated with Maud Oakes and Jeff King on *Where the Two Came to Their Father: A Navajo War Ceremonial*, Bollingen Series I, in two volumes (text and plates). He had previously collaborated with Henry Morton Robinson on *A Skeleton Key to Finnegans Wake*, also published in 1943, before the publication of his own breakaway book, *The Hero with a Thousand Faces*, in 1949. He devoted much of the rest of the 1940s, as well as half of the 1950s, to the editing and posthumous publication of the papers of Heinrich Zimmer, who had died suddenly in 1943. The resulting books include *Myths and Symbols in Indian Art and Civilization* (1946), *The King and the Corpse* (1948), *Philosophies of India* (1951), and the monumental, two-volume *The Arts of Indian Asia* (1955). Subsequently, Campbell turned his attention to writing his own series, *The Masks of God*, published in four volumes between 1959 and 1968.

All of these publications came during a very rich "Golden Age" of mythological studies in the United States, with important works of comparative studies published by preeminent scholars in literature and religious studies—many of whom Campbell knew and who provided endorsement and support of his work. For a glimpse into his conversations with such figures as Mircea

Eliade, Henri Corbin, Ananda K. Coomaraswamy, Heinrich Zimmer, and Thomas Mann, see *Correspondence: 1927–1987* (New World Library, 2019), a collection of Campbell's letters that Dennis Patrick Slattery, PhD, and I edited. I highly recommend the books of the aforementioned authors as further reading that supplements this study guide, as do Campbell's other publications and lectures, which are available from the Joseph Campbell Foundation (jcf.org).

The Flight of the Wild Gander can be seen as a book at the crossroads of Campbell's career—a summation of where he had been and an indication of where he was headed. And indeed, in that latter sense, the book is an overture to the grand opera to come—stating its major themes and announcing lifelong preoccupations that would be developed in his many books that followed. Those themes and concerns are announced in Campbell's own "Introduction" to the book: folklore and mythology, theology and philosophy, shamanism and depth psychology, the mythologies of the Neolithic Near East, the Paleolithic caves of Europe, the Native American visions of Black Elk, and the Grail Romances of the Middle Ages. As an overture, therefore, the book is an excellent introduction to Campbell's work, with concise statements of those motifs to be elaborately amplified in the second half of his career. It offers a menu, you might say, of the extraordinary banquet to come. It provides an excellent foundation for teaching or taking any course concerned with myth and religious studies from a transdisciplinary perspective—one which would include theology, philosophy, cultural studies, literature, and the arts. If you are new to such studies, or if you are looking back on a career greatly enriched by Campbell's life and work, I can only say, "Here beginneth the marvels!" Above all, enjoy the feast.

Skeleton Key Study Guide Introduction

NOTES

1 Friedrich Hölderlin, *Hyperion*, Volume 1, Book 1, "Hyperion to Bellarmin [IV]."

Introduction

Chapter Summary

The Introduction chapter serves as a brief overture to the opera that is *The Flight of the Wild Gander*, stating the main themes and motifs in the essays that follow. In many ways, the book itself is a useful overture to Campbell's entire body of work, summarizing and anticipating key themes that he amplifies later. Indeed, the first paragraph summarizes the primary motivation of his work to date: "The writing of the following essays," he states, "occupied, or rather punctuated, a period of twenty-four years, during the whole course of which I was circling, and from many quarters striving to interpret, the mystery of mythology: to lift the veil, so to say, of that Goddess of the ancient temple of Saïs who could say with truth, and can say today, and will say to the end of time, 'no one has lifted my veil.'"[1]

Campbell's reference to Saïs is significant: It refers to a time in Ancient Greece during the last few centuries BCE when the mythologies of the ancient world (both Greek and Egyptian) were being interpreted through the lens of the Neoplatonic philosophers such as Plutarch (46–119 CE). Plutarch's essay "Isis and Osiris" tells us that the shrine of the Goddess at Saïs (Athena, whom he associates with Isis) carried the inscription, "I am all that hath been, and is, and shall be; and my veil no mortal has hitherto raised." This synthesis of Greek and Egyptian mythology laid the foundation for what would become Campbell's version of a fully comparative mythology, which embraces all of the mythologies of the world—though without applying a specifically Platonic lens to their interpretation.

Campbell's intentions for *Wild Gander* as a whole appear in his statement about the purpose of its first chapter, "The Fairy Tale," which, he writes, "is intended here to introduce the whole problem of the fascination, sources, preservation, and interpretation of those dreamlike images and narratives that reappear in more impressive dress in the holy scriptures both of the Orient and of the Occident, as well as in our higher secular arts."[2] In other words, fairy tales have more in common with scripture than we might think at first glance.

With regard to the second essay, "Bios and Mythos," Campbell states his "basic thesis—that myths are a function of nature, as well as of culture, and as necessary to the balanced maturation of the human psyche as is nourishment to the whole body."[3] Myth feeds our souls as food feeds our bodies.

He further clarifies his intentions by remarking that the next essay in the book, "Primitive Man as Metaphysician," argues for the "release of the archetypal symbolic images of mythic thought from their various local matrices of culturally conditioned references and 'meaning,' so that [...] they may be recognized in themselves as natural phenomena, opening backward to mystery—like trees, like hills, or like mountain streams—antecedent (like the wood of trees) to the 'meanings' that have been given them and the uses to which they have been put."[4] This is an elegant way of saying that the images we see in mythology can point beyond themselves to deeper, more profound meanings than they seem to have on the surface.

Campbell then indicates his inclination to apply depth psychology to the interpretation of myth by stating that "dream and vision have been, everywhere and forever, the chief creative and

"Living myths are not mistaken notions, and they do not spring from books. They are not to be judged as true or false but as effective or ineffective, maturative or pathogenic."

—THE FLIGHT OF THE WILD GANDER, *page xiv*

shaping powers of myth."⁵ Depth psychology, which is different from contemporary research psychology, focuses more on individual psychological images and meaning than on experiments, data, and statistics. That's why Campbell cites the work of the founders of depth psychology, Sigmund Freud (1856–1939) and Carl G. Jung (1875–1961). Like myth, Freud writes, the dream-wish emerges from the "unknown," from "some denser part" of the psyche, "like the mushroom from its mycelium."⁶ Jung argues that "we may expect to find in dreams everything that has ever been of significance in the life of humanity," and that "(i)n order to do justice to dreams, we need an interpretive equipment that must be laboriously fitted together from all branches of the humane sciences."⁷ Campbell, more than any other commentator on mythology in our times, has risen to this challenge in all his books, which apply depth psychology, anthropology, archaeology, philosophy, literature, and the arts to understanding the meaning and importance of myth.

Those myths change, however, and their meanings change with them. It is particularly urgent to address such changes during a period like our own, which is filled with what Campbell sees as "outdated mythic teachings."⁸ Under these circumstances, it is no one myth that we need, but rather "the living source of all myths."⁹ And all of those myths serve both a psychological function, addressing the healthy development of the psyche, and a "metaphysical, or mystagogic function [...] opening backward to mystery."¹⁰ The term "mystery" here doesn't mean a puzzle to be solved, but rather the unknowable source from which all of existence springs, along with our myths.

In the fourth chapter, "Mythogenesis," Campbell tells us he will turn from the natural, biological, and psychological dimensions

"Not the promise of any given myth or the claims of any inherited god but the living source of all myths and of all the gods and their worlds is what today is holy and to be sought..."

—THE FLIGHT OF THE WILD GANDER, *page xiv*

Introduction

"to the cultural, historical aspect of the rise, flowering, and decline of a mythology."[11] Entire mythologies have beginnings, middles, and ends, just like the stories they contain.

The penultimate chapter, called "The Symbol Without Meaning," further addresses what Campbell calls "the mythological dimension," this time incorporating findings from archaeology which were new at the time he was writing.

Finally, the last chapter, "The Secularization of the Sacred," addresses a cultural conflict between Europe's focus on individual creativity and Asia's emphasis on the needs of the group.

NOTES

1 Campbell, *The Flight of the Wild Gander: Explorations in the Mythological Dimension*, xi.
2 Ibid, xi.
3 Ibid, xi.
4 Ibid, xii.
5 Ibid, xii.
6 Ibid, quoted on xii.
7 Ibid, quoted on xiii.
8 Ibid, xiii.
9 Ibid, xiv.
10 Ibid, xv.
11 Ibid, xv.

Chapter I
The Fairy Tale

Chapter Summary

THE WORK OF THE BROTHERS GRIMM

Jacob (1785–1863) and Wilhelm (1786–1859) Grimm collected stories for their famous work from a variety of sources, such as Katherina Viehmann (1755–1815). Storytellers like Viehmann relayed the tales out loud and could tell them slowly enough that the brothers could write them down word for word.

The Grimms' interest in these tales began when Jacob found a collection of love poems by the Minnesinger poets of the twelfth and thirteenth centuries in the library of Friedrich von Savigny. This discovery came at the time of the so-called German Romantic movement, which was deeply engaged in the study of myth and folk tale, as evidenced by Johann Gottfried Herder's *Folk Songs* (1778–79). These songs inspired Goethe's interest in folk ballads such as *"Der Erlkönig"* ("The Elf King"), as well as Clemens Brentano's and Achim von Arnim's 1805 collection of German folk songs, *Des Knabens Wunderhorn* (The Child's Wonder Horn). In the transcription and writing of the tales Wilhelm was inspired by popular modes of speech and "typical manners of descriptive narrative,"[1] which led him to chisel away abstract, literary, or colorless language.

"Myth, as the psychoanalysts declare, is not a mess of errors; myth is a picture language. But the language has to be studied to be read."

—THE FLIGHT OF THE WILD GANDER, *page 22*

Chapter I: The Fairy Tale

Campbell provides a helpful chronology for publications of the tales:

- 1806: Napoleonic armies overrun Kassel.

- 1808: Jacob is appointed superintendent of the private library of Jérôme Bonaparte, puppet King of Westphalia.

- 1812: Napoleon retreats from Moscow; Volume One of *Kinder und Haus-Märchen* is published (and banned as superstition in Vienna).

- 1815: Volume Two of the tales is published.

- 1819: The second edition of the tales is published, with a new introduction by Wilhelm entitled "On the Nature of Folk Tales."

- 1822: Volume Three is published, with a commentary and thorough comparative-historical study.

- 1825: A collection of the brothers' fifty favorite tales is published.

- 1837: The third edition of the two-volume original is published.

- 1842, 1843, 1850, 1857: Further editions are published, as well as translations of the stories into many languages.

THE TYPES OF STORY

After the first volume of tales appeared, scholars immediately began following in the Grimms' footsteps. Field workers transcribed tales as precisely as they could from informants all over the world. Campbell classifies these tales into three main types:

- *Myths*—religious stories told not for entertainment but for spiritual teaching.

- *Legends*—stories that combine history with myth.

- *Tales*—stories told for entertainment, such as animal tales, fairy tales, and heroic or romantic adventures. Tales can include myths or legends from earlier times that people don't fully believe in anymore.

Stories often open and close with recognizable formulas such as "Once upon a time" and "They lived happily ever after." Stories are mostly told in prose, but sometimes also include poetry and rhyme. However, some stories—such as bardic lays, epics, and ballads—are recounted entirely in poetry.

Campbell also describes three other types of story:

- *Anecdotes*—stories of personal experience that could be true or made up.

- *Inventions*—jokes, merry tales, and ghost stories.

- *Fables*—teaching tales that dramatize a truism or moral point.

The Grimms included all these tale types in their collections. Other scholars have created tale classifications. The Appendix of *Flight of the Wild Gander* includes a listing of tale types based on the work of Finnish folklorist Antti Aarne (1867–1925).

THE HISTORY OF THE TALES

Interest in the Grimm Brothers' tales was fueled by nationalist movements of the time, when the French had defeated Germany during the Napoleonic wars. The Grimms understood the tales as retaining the "detritus of Old Germanic belief: the myths of Ancient time had disintegrated, first into heroic legend and romance, last into the folk tales."[2] That would mean that German tales should hold clues to an ancient German religion. But in 1859 Theodor Benfey's collection of Sanskrit tales, the *Panchatantra*, gave rise to a truly global form of comparative mythology and folk tales by demonstrating "that a great portion of the lore of Europe had come, through Arabic, Hebrew, and Latin translations, directly from India."[3] So these German tales also held clues to many kinds of ancient religious thought.

At the end of the 1800s, some English scholars believed that "irrational" (meaning impossible or unreal) elements in fairy tales came from beliefs that predate the scientific understanding of the world. But people who understand the world scientifically encounter "irrational" elements as well, such as in their dreams. Instead of throwing out irrationalities, we can view them as metaphors to discover surprising new meanings.

Campbell next provides an overview of the history of the transmission of stories in Europe:

Chapter I: The Fairy Tale

- In the tenth century, traveling entertainers imported Greek and Roman story material from the Mediterranean.

- In the twelfth century, story content from India reached Europe thanks to the Crusades, and the rise of Arthurian Romances brought Celtic material from Ireland into the mix.

- In the thirteenth century, the Hindu *Panchatantra* arrived. This book of stories was translated from Sanskrit into Persian in the sixth century, from Hebrew into Latin by John of Capua in 1270, from which it passed into German and Italian. A Spanish translation appeared from an Arabic version in 1251, then came an English version from the Italian. Individual tales become popular and then found their way into European traditions.

- Also in the thirteenth century, prose collections of traditional lore began appearing, much of which also appeared in the literature of the Late Middle Ages, Reformation, and the Renaissance.

- In the seventeenth-century court of Louis XIV, new French translations of the *Panchatantra* and the Arabian *Thousand Nights and One Night* inspired new versions of fairy tales and fables. I would add that these collections were of great importance for the rise of the English novel, in the works of Fielding, Swift, and Johnson.

So, by the time the Grimms were collecting their traditional tales, a wealth of different influences had mingled to create the versions that they transcribed. As a story travels from place to place, it changes in many ways, but it also retains what Campbell calls its "key-complex,"[4] or an essential idea without which it would be a completely different story.

The study of stories began in Europe with the Romantics, matured with the Grimms, and then became systemized in 1907 in Finland as an expression of nationalistic pride. Members of the Finnish School used the "geographical-historical method" of retracing the path of an individual tale "practically to the doorstep of its inventor."[5]

Elias Lonnröt (1802–84), a country doctor, collected ballads and folk tales to produce the *Kalevala*, the "folk epic of Finland." Julius Krohn (1835–88), however, concluded that the collected tales were not originally Finnish, but rather had migrated northwards from the Mediterranean via the Slavs and Tatars. Then, in 1911, Antti Aarne produced his prodigious index of folk tale types, brought up to date in 1928 by Stith Thompson. This index is now recognized as an invaluable resource for the study of folk tale types from around the world.

In Germany and Finland, the gathering of local lore began out of local patriotism, but quickly became the study of the worldwide influences on individual stories and the many different versions of each story.

THE QUESTION OF MEANING

The meaning and interpretation of myths and folk tales was an obsession of the philosophers, poets, artists, and musicians of

"Myths, therefore, as they now come to us, … are the purveyors of a wisdom that has borne the race of man through the long vicissitudes of his career."

—THE FLIGHT OF THE WILD GANDER, *page 22–23*

the Romantic movement, both in Germany and in England. It is a hotly debated field of inquiry still today, with many influential theorists engaged in the fray. In his commentary, Campbell provides a brief overview of the field.

THE MOTIFS

For the Greek Euhemerus (fourth century BCE), the myths of the gods were based on legendary exploits of historical figures such as Alexander the Great, who were deified after their deaths.

For the German Romantic linguist Max Müller, myth and folk tale were rooted in descriptions of nature, particularly in the daily and yearly cycles of the sun. This focus produced the so-called solar hero, such as Gawain in the Arthurian Romances. (Note: This notion would later be adapted as the "night-sea journey" by Leo Frobenius, whose work profoundly influenced both C.G. Jung and Joseph Campbell.)

In England, the Cambridge school of anthropologists was inspired by Sir James George Frazer's encyclopedic study of myth, *The Golden Bough*. In Frazer's view, myths were attempts to explain the world. Of particular importance for Campbell was Jane Ellen Harrison's *Prolegomena to the Study of Greek Religion*, in which she argues that myths are rooted in grave cults and the fear of death. (In the same book, Harrison develops an idea that would be of central importance to Campbell throughout his life and work, i.e., that the patriarchal pantheon of Homeric gods was preceded by the centrality of female divinities, such as Demeter and Persephone.)

Campbell then brings the conversation about the meaning of myth and folk tales forward, beginning with the sociologist Émile Durkheim, for whom the essence of religious ritual was the communal, shared, social experience of sacred power transmitted by physical objects called totems. This became a platform for the sociological study of myth—central to the French schools, but not to Campbell's liking. He was more drawn to the emerging school of psychoanalysis, particularly the work of Freud and Jung, both of whom he greatly admired and cited frequently. For these early "depth psychologists," "(t)he monstrous, irrational and unnatural" motifs of myth and folk tale emerge from dreams and the unconscious psyche.[6]

Campbell also points out that poets, prophets, priests, and other visionaries from all over the world have used the images of myth to articulate and share spiritual wisdom.

THE TALES

Unlike myths, tales are crafted by tellers whose goal is to entertain. At their best, tale tellers used symbols of the wonders of the spirit. In other words, tales were never meant to be believed. Myths, on the other hand, *were* meant to be believed. While belief in myths might come and go as empirical knowledge changes, tales that demand no belief can endure. What's more, these tales remain full of symbolism of the human psyche. This deeper dimension of folk tale and mythic motifs survives in visionary literature and music, such as in the works of Blake, Wagner, Strindberg, Nietzsche, Melville, Joyce, and Mann. Fairy tales themselves live on as well.

Chapter I: The Fairy Tale

One can see in this concise discussion of the meaning of the tales the beginnings of the "four functions" of mythology that Campbell would later develop as a cornerstone of his work, beginning with *The Masks of God: Creative Mythology*. The first of these four functions—and to Campbell the most important—is the mystical (myths as stories that reconcile us to the awe-inspiring reality behind or beyond our day-to-day perceptions). The second is the cosmological (myths as an image of the universe and its natural cycles). The third is the socio-political (myths that enforce moral order and the foundational ideologies of a culture). The fourth function is the psychological (myths as narrative expressions of the stages of human life and development).

COMPLEMENTARY READING FROM CAMPBELL'S WORK

This chapter of *Flight of the Wild Gander* was first published as a commentary essay in *Grimm's Fairytales: Complete Edition*, by Pantheon Books in 1944. In 1947, Campbell's posthumous edition of Heinrich Zimmer's *The King and the Corpse* would include analyses of the Persian tale, "Abu Kasem's Slippers" and the marvelous Sanskrit tale of the book's title. Two years later, in 1949, would come Campbell's breakthrough book, *The Hero with a Thousand Faces*, which includes discussions of many folk tales from around the world.

An abundance of tales is also to be found in Campbell's edition of *The Portable Arabian Nights* (1952), which includes his rich introduction to the collection. That introduction now opens *The Thousand and One Nights*, a volume in the *Collected Works of Joseph Campbell*.

All volumes of *The Historical Atlas of World Mythology* offer a rich panorama of world mythology and folk tales from many cultural traditions.

Further Reading

Bettelheim, Bruno. *The Uses of Enchantment*. Alfred A. Knopf, 1976.

Bly, Robert. *Iron John*. Addison Wesley, 1999.

Tatar, Maria. *Classic Fairy Tales*, 2d ed. Norton Critical Editions, 2016.

Zipes, Jack. *The Great Fairy Tale Tradition*. W.W. Norton & Company, 2000.

—. *The Complete Fairy Tales of the Brothers Grimm*, 3d ed. Bantam, 2003.

—. *Spells of Enchantment: The Wondrous Fairy Tales of Western Culture*. Penguin, 1992.

The Pantheon Fairy Tale and Folklore Library, any volume.

Von Franz, Marie-Louise. *Individuation in Fairy Tales*. Shambhala, 1991.

—. *Shadow and Evil in Fairy Tales*. Shambhala, 1995.

—. *The Interpretation of Fairy Tales*. Shambhala, 1996.

—. *The Feminine in Fairy Tales*. Shambhala, 2001.

"Playful and unpretentious as the archetypes of fairy tale may appear to be, they are the heroes and villains who have built the world for us."

—THE FLIGHT OF THE WILD GANDER, *page 24*

Discussion and Essay Questions

- Choose a traditional fairy tale you are particularly fond of and reflect on the story's meaning, using one or more of the interpretations of the material Campbell discusses in this section.

- Choose a contemporary version of a fairy tale (film, graphic novel, comic book, retelling) and reflect on how it offers new perspectives on the story.

- Contrast the approaches to fairy tales using such theoretical writings as those by Marie-Louise von Franz, Bruno Bettelheim, Jack Zipes, and Maria Tatar.

Creative Prompts

- Write your own version of a traditional fairy tale, in prose or verse form.

- Create an artwork based on one of the tales (drawing, painting, sculpture, weaving, film script, etc.)

- Write an entirely original, "new" story in the tradition of the folk tales.

NOTES

1 Campbell, *The Flight of the Wild Gander: Explorations in the Mythological Dimension*, 5.
2 Ibid, 11.
3 Ibid, 11.
4 Ibid, 14.
5 Ibid, 15.
6 Ibid, 23.

Chapter II
Bios and Mythos

Chapter Summary

SOCIOLOGICAL AND PSYCHOLOGICAL SCHOOLS OF INTERPRETATION

The archetypes, or repeating motifs, of mythology are easy to recognize. For example, Catholic colonizers of the Americas saw similarities to their religion in the sacred stories and rituals of indigenous First Nations people. Campbell quotes a story gathered from Father Pedro Simon's mission in seventeenth century Colombia, in which there was a prophecy that the sun would incarnate in the womb of a virgin. So two sisters went to a mountaintop in hopes of attracting the attention of the sun. One of them conceived and gave birth to an emerald, which she put between her breasts. The emerald changed into baby whom she named Goranchacho, "Child of the Sun." While Father Simon recognized the parallels to the Virgin Birth of Jesus in this myth, he saw the indigenous story as the devil's work.

Campbell's discussion of the schools of interpretation begins with Adolph Bastian (1826–1905), an anthropologist who traveled in China, Japan, India, Africa, and South America. Bastian coined two dialectical terms that Campbell would frequently refer to his books: On the one hand, certain ideas recur throughout world mythology; these archetypal ideas Bastian calls *Elementargedanken* (Elementary Ideas). On the other hand, story elements unique to a particular place he calls *Völkergedanken* (Ethnic [or Folk] Ideas). The notion was that the most basic structures of the human imagination are as universal

"Mythology is the womb of mankind's initiation to life and death."

—THE FLIGHT OF THE WILD GANDER, *page 34*

as the organs of the body, but that these elementary forms are clothed in different cultural languages and traditions.

Campbell points out that scholars such as Edward Tyler, Sir James George Frazer, Franz Boas, and other comparative mythologists of the nineteenth and twentieth centuries also saw similarities in myths from around the world. In the first edition of *The Mind of Primitive Man* (1911), for example, Franz Boas wrote that "in the main the mental characteristics of man are the same all over the world," and that "certain patterns of associated ideas may be recognized in all types of culture."[1] To Campbell's dismay, this statement was deleted in the second edition, as the tide of academic discourse shifted to focusing on the differences between cultures. Campbell vigorously attacks this approach, which he calls "Durkheimian myopia," contrasting it with the "sundry schools of the diffusionists, stressing cultural affinities that obviously unite vast portions of the human race."[2] Campbell sides firmly with those who see consistency between different cultures' myths and folk tales.

He then lists several possible origins for the emergence of world mythologies, including the Indo-Europeans, Mesopotamia, Egypt, and Syria, plus diffusions across the Pacific Ocean from China and Japan, pointing out that "Mythological archetypes (Bastian's Elementary Ideas) cut across the boundaries of these culture spheres."[3] The primary problem, therefore, "is not historical or ethnological, but psychological—even biological,"[4] meaning that the forms of myth arise from the deeper, more fundamental nature of humankind rather than culture.

Campbell sees poets, artists, and romantic philosophers who work with myth as an important complement to academic discourse, because mythology is a source of "life-awakening" images, rooted in our biology, forming a "picture language of metaphysics" and the "soul."[5] But Campbell also sees promise for a "science of myth" in the field of depth psychology, because of Sigmund Freud's and C.G. Jung's recognition of the kinship between myth and dream.

THE BIOLOGICAL FUNCTION OF MYTH

Some scholars believe that culture itself originates in humankind's long period of infancy, when a baby is completely dependent on adults for food and protection. Adults, in turn, are dependent on society for their food and protection. Campbell sees society as a "second womb,"[6] a system of "symbolic potentialities"[7] that protects the psyche. Some of these symbols come from within the individual, and some come from the outside environment.

(The psyche needs protection in part from what Rudolf Otto in his influential book *The Idea of the Holy* called the *mysterium tremendum* of the numinous power of the divine energies, from which all mythology and all religion derives. As Jung would have it, the function of religion is to protect us from an experience of God!)

In Campbell's view, myth provides a symbolic mode of mastering inner and outer reality. The commonality of myth and ritual revolves around what James Joyce (in his novel *A Portrait of the Artist as a Young Man*) called "the grave and constant in human sufferings"[8]—such as birth, adolescence, marriage, death, and rebirth.

THE IMAGE OF A SECOND BIRTH

Rituals such as the Christian Eucharist combine with myth to create the "second womb" of culture.[9] In many traditions, the whole idea is to be born a second time, that is, from this cultural womb. In India, being born again through myth results in spiritual freedom—freedom from myth and other cultural constraints. In Christianity, baptism is a birth of the spirit, but the Christian tradition resists the idea of leaving myth behind.

The archetypal theme of death and rebirth recurs in Neoplatonic and Taoist philosophies; in the Greek Mysteries; in the myths and rites of Phoenicia, Mesopotamia, and Egypt; as well as among the Celts, Germans, Aztecs, and Mayans. Campbell cites the anthropologist Géza Roheim who suggested that "Death and rebirth are the typical contents of all initiation rites,"[10] a notion that would be further developed by religious historian and author Mircea Eliade, Campbell's friend and colleague from the University of Chicago. Campbell supports this claim by citing imagery that appears in the bull-roarers of the Keraki people in contemporary New Guinea, and in European burials and cave paintings from tens of thousands of years ago. Myth, he says, "is everywhere the womb of man's specifically human birth."[11] The images and stories of myth allow us to be born into our spiritual selves.

THE ANXIETY OF THE MISBORN

Campbell concludes this chapter with the critical insight that "five hundred years of systematic dismemberment and rejection of the mythological organ of our species" has created our psychological, spiritual, and social problems.[12] Without myth, we

"Rites, then, together with the mythologies that support them, constitute the second womb, the matrix of the postnatal gestation of the placental Homo sapiens."

—THE FLIGHT OF THE WILD GANDER, *page 37–38*

lack effective rites of passage. Poets and artists, however, can reclaim their "traditional function of seer and mystagogue of the regenerative vision."[13] In effect, literature and art can offer images that function the way myth does.

COMPLEMENTARY READING FROM CAMPBELL'S WORK

For further material on Campbell's interest in Jung, see his introduction to *The Portable Jung* (Viking Press, 1973).

For more about Campbell's interest in Freud, see the index references in *The Hero with a Thousand Faces* and *The Masks of God*. See also the episode entitled "Psyche and Symbol" from the video series, *Mythos I: The Shaping of Our Mythic Tradition*.

For the work of Bastian and Bachofen, see Campbell's introduction to *Myth, Religion, & Mother Right: Selected Writings of J. J. Bachofen* (Princeton UP, 1992), and also "Prologue: Myth and the Body" in *The Inner Reaches of Outer Space*. See also Campbell's edited volume from the Eranos Yearbooks entitled *The Mysteries* (Princeton UP, 1979).

FURTHER READING

Eliade, Mircea. *Rites and Symbols of Initiation: The Mysteries of Death and Rebirth*. Spring Publications, 1998.

Otto, Rudolf. *The Idea of the Holy*, Trans. John Harvey. Oxford University Press, 1958.

"The same idea of the 'second birth' is certainly basic to Christianity also, where it is symbolized in baptism."

—THE FLIGHT OF THE WILD GANDER, *page 38*

Discussion and Essay Questions

- Discuss any form of initiation ritual—for example, a religious ceremony, fraternity or sorority induction, athletic or military contest, rock concert, graduation, or other event—that seems to invoke a death and rebirth experience. Reflect upon its relevance to the unfolding of your life.
- Choose a ritual from literature, the arts, mythological traditions, or music, and then write an essay that addresses its universal and particular cultural-specific themes.

Creative Prompt

Create your own version of a ritual, and imagine how that might be performed with a group.

NOTES

1 Campbell, *The Flight of the Wild Gander: Explorations in the Mythological Dimension*, 29.
2 Ibid, 30.
3 Ibid, 31.
4 Ibid, 31.
5 Ibid, 32.
6 Ibid, 36.
7 Ibid, 35.
8 Ibid, 37.
9 Ibid, 37.
10 Ibid, 39.
11 Ibid, 40.
12 Ibid, 41.
13 Ibid, 41.

Chapter III
Primitive Man as Metaphysician

Chapter Summary

TENDER- AND TOUGH-MINDED THINKING

The title of the opening section of this chapter refers to a debate among anthropologists regarding the study and interpretation of myth. Some anthropologists focus on similarities between cultures, and some focus on the unique particularities of each culture. The argument is clearly illustrated by two editions of a book called *The Mind of Primitive Man*, by Franz Boas, the founder of American anthropology. Campbell points out that in the first edition, of 1911, Boas wrote, "The metaphysical notions of man may be reduced to a few types which are of universal distribution."[1] This sentence did not appear in the second edition, of 1938, when the focus had shifted from the study of "common features" shared by many mythologies to the particular differences between them—a view that came to dominate the field. In the early 1950s, however, "the tide again had turned," as indicated by the title of such important articles as Clyde Kluckhorn's on "The Universal Categories of Culture."[2]

Even before then, some thirty years earlier, Paul Radin had suggested reconciling the two points of view in his book *Primitive Man as Philosopher*. Campbell summarizes Radin's description of the conflict as one between "the tough-minded and tender-minded."[3] To the tough-minded, facts do not have symbolic value. The tender-minded, however, are interested in deeper meanings, causes, and implications of facts. In anthropology,

"Unless the myths can be understood—or felt—to be true in some such way as this, they lose their force, their magic, their charm…"

—THE FLIGHT OF THE WILD GANDER, *page 52*

Chapter III: Primitive Man as Metaphysician

the tough-minded focus on the details of differences between cultures, while the tender-minded focus on the "universal distribution" of key themes shared by many myths.[4] At the time of the publication of this essay in 1960, American anthropologists tended to be tough-minded, so Campbell's intention here is to offer an alternative view for scholars exclusively focused on cultural differences.

THE IMAGE AND ITS MEANING

To lay the foundations of this alternative view, this section establishes the difference between symbols and the metaphysical ideas they refer to. Symbols such as those proposed by Franz Boas—a land of the souls of the dead, for example, or many worlds—Campbell argues, are images, not metaphysical ideas.

Metaphysics transcends ideas like these. Metaphysical realizations refer to an awareness that lies outside of space, time, and all the known things of everyday. The next section discusses mythological images which point to a shared metaphysical realization.

IMAGERY OF THE MANIFOLD AND ITS "CAUSE"

This section lists a series of mythological images that describe the creation of the world in different ways.

The first example was collected by Natalie Curtis, in *The Indians' Book*, published in 1907. In this myth, a man emerges from a place where the darkness crowds together and then separates. From his body, the man draws out a stick and then creates ants (also from his body) which he puts on the end of the stick, where they make a round ball from the gum of the wood. The man takes the ball of gum from the stick and puts it down in the darkness in front of him, and stands upon it, rolling it around under his feet while singing. By singing and rolling the ball he creates the world, bringing rocks out of his body that he turns into stars, followed by the creation of the Milky Way, the moon, and finally the sun. This last proves the most difficult: The man has to make two large bowls, filling one with water and covering it over with the other, so that he can sit watching the bowls, while wishing for his creation to happen. And so the sun is born from his wish. He throws the sun to the east, the north, the west, and to the south. Each time it remains motionless in the sky, until he throws it again to the east, where it bounces up into the sky and begins to move.

A second origin myth comes from the Sanskrit Brihadāranyaka Upanishad, in which all things begin with a person in the shape of a man. He is lonely and wants a mate, so he swells and then divides into two people, a man and a woman, from whom the first people are born. The woman then hides herself and takes the forms of a cow, a mare, a donkey, a goat, a ewe. He follows, taking the forms of a bull, a stallion, a male donkey, a buck, and a ram to mate with her in each form, so that cattle, horses, goats and sheep can be born. And so it goes all the way down to the ants. After that heroic sequence of copulations, the primordial being knows itself as the Creation of all the forms of the world.

Campbell then provides a rather staggering list of origin myths, to illustrate the theme of the "Manifold," or the many, that comes from the "One," or a single, mysterious, unknowable source.[5] These myths include Ymir from the Icelandic Eddas, who creates Rime-Giants from his hands, and then is cut to pieces by the

"Wherever myths still are living symbols, the mythologies are teeming dream worlds of such images."

—THE FLIGHT OF THE WILD GANDER, *page 53*

younger generation of gods (Wotan, Will, and We) in order to be transformed into rocks and mountains and lakes and sky and all the rest of creation. In the Babylonian *Epic of Creation*, the hero Marduk cuts up the body of the monster Tiamat, whose parts are fashioned into the forms of the universe (the Tigris and Euphrates rivers streaming from her eyes like tears). Egyptian myth gives us the god Ptah, from whom all the gods come forth (sometimes by the power of the word, and sometimes by shaping the world on a potter's wheel). Much later, in Ovid's *Metamorphoses*, the creation is a more abstract affair, in which an unnamed god brings order out of chaos. In India's highly philosophical metaphysical system called Vedanta, the universe comes from a primordial entity that is a fusion of consciousness, or awareness, and ignorance, or the lack of awareness.

Campbell suggests that all these myths express a single thought: that somehow, the One becomes the many. No myth explains exactly how it happens because this mystery is unknowable. No matter how the myths represent the "primordial One."[6] it remains essentially beyond our comprehension and articulation. It remains a mystery.

THE "CAUSE" UNDERSTOOD AS ABSOLUTELY UNKNOWN

Campbell summarizes Immanuel Kant's formula and examples for interpreting metaphysical symbols. This formula takes the form of an analogy: *a* is to *b* as *c* is to *x*, where *x* is something that cannot be known. While we can't know the nature of *x*, we can infer something about it from observing its effects (the creation of the world), and comparing that to other known effects and their causes. For example, the same way parents help their children find happiness (*a*) because of the parents' love for the children (*b*), the well-being of humankind (*c*) comes from God's unknowable love (*x*). Also, the same way that the first, unknowable cause of creation relates to the world, human thinking relates to human artwork.

The symbolic images of myth represent analogies of a relationship between something known and mystery that is unknowable. This mystery can only be approximated—never fully known—by these comparisons.

THEOLOGY AS A MISREADING OF MYTHOLOGY

When the sense of mystery in a myth can no longer be felt, the stories and images lose their vitality and become mere artifacts from the past. Theological dogmas and belief systems must therefore be reductive, and in fact delusional, if they take themselves to be the final terms of their analogies. For such images as God, Jahweh, Jesus, and Vishnu point beyond themselves "to their universal, transcendental" essence—which, as the previous section suggested, must remain elusive. We can only intuit those divine energies; they cannot be reduced to intellectual systems. If they are, the "living symbols" lose their efficacy, and must die in order to be transformed and integrated into new mythologies.

To illustrate how these figures point to the mystery of their "metaphysical essence,"[7] Campbell cites the *Bhagavad Gītā*, the hero mythology of the Jicarilla Apache tribe of New Mexico, the Greek tragedian Aeschylus, and the Sioux medicine man Black Elk. In the *Bhagavad Gītā*, Krishna states that "Neither the hosts of gods, nor the great saints, know my origin [....] I am the Self existing in the heart of all beings: I am the beginning, the middle, and also the end of all beings."[8] (These words recall Jesus of the Apocalypse, who in Revelation 22:13 declares "I am Alpha and Omega, the beginning and the end, the first and the last," or indeed those of Isis of Saïs, whose inscription reads: "I am all that hath been, and is, and shall be; and my veil no mortal has hitherto raised.")

In the Jicarilla Apache myth, the hero Killer of Enemies says to his people "The earth is my body. The sky is my body. The seasons are my body. The water is my body too."[9] Aeschylus wrote, "Zeus is air, Zeus is earth, Zeus is heaven; / Zeus is all things, and whatsoever is higher than all things."[10] Campbell concludes his examples with Black Elk, who said "all things are the works of the Great Spirit. We should know that He is within all things: the trees, the grasses, the rivers, the mountains, and all the four-legged animals, and the winged peoples; and even more important, we should understand that He is also above all these things and people."[11]

When myth functions as a set of "living symbols,"[12] Campbell concludes, the stories are full of these vibrant metaphysical images. But when a myth is reduced to a systematic theology, and read literally as history or science, then the symbols are mistaken for facts, and metaphor for dogma, giving rise to conflicts between different religions and belief systems, each of which confuses its own symbols for the metaphysical mystery to which they point.

Chapter III: Primitive Man as Metaphysician

ESOTERIC AND EXOTERIC ANTHROPOLOGY

In this final section, Campbell concludes with the dialectic between the tough-minded and the tender-minded which is central to this entire chapter, clearly restating his preference for the latter—without, it must be said, rejecting the former.

Esoteric teaching refers to the tender-minded emphasis on symbolic meanings, while exoteric doctrine is the tough-minded emphasis on literal facts. Campbell poses the question of where mythology comes from: artistic tender minds, or no-nonsense tough minds? For him, mythologies emerge from "the poetical imagery of the tender-minded," and are then misapprehended by "the clumsy misreadings" of tough-minded anthropologists and theologians.[13]

It is the tender-minded who have played "the chief role in the significant shaping of traditions, since it is everywhere the priests and shamans who have maintained and developed the general inheritance of myths and symbols."[14] In other words, Campbell sees the spiritual leaders who work most closely with myths as experts in esoteric teachings. What is needed, therefore, in the study of myth, is to move from a dialectic to a dialogue between the opposing points of view.

NOTABLE QUOTES

"For the bedrock of the science of folklore and myth is not in the wisps and strays of metaphor, but in the ideas to which the metaphors refer." —*The Flight of the Wild Gander*, page 56

"For myself, I believe that we owe both the imagery and the poetical insights of myth to the genius of the tender-minded; to the tough-minded only their reduction to religion."

—THE FLIGHT OF THE WILD GANDER, *page 55*

Chapter III: Primitive Man as Metaphysician

COMPLEMENTARY READING FROM CAMPBELL'S WORK

For more about Campbell's views on early mythologies, see *The Historical Atlas of World Mythology: The Way of the Animal Powers* (Harper Collins, 1988).

For more about his views of myth, symbol, and metaphor, see *The Inner Reaches of Outer Space: Metaphor as Myth and as Religion* from *The Collected Works of Joseph Campbell* (New World Library, 2012).

FURTHER READING

Eliot, Alexander. *Universal Myths: Heroes, Gods, Tricksters, and Others.* Meridian, 1990.

Fontenrose, Joseph. *Python: A Study of the Delphic Myth and Its Origin.* University of CA Press, 1980.

Hamilton, Virginia. *In the Beginning: Creation Stories from Around the World*, Illus. Barry Moser. Turtleback, 1997.

Sproul, Barbara. *Primal Myths: Creation Myths Around the World.* Harper & Row, 1991.

Von Franz, Marie-Louise. *Creation Myths.* Shambhala, 2017.

DISCUSSION AND ESSAY QUESTIONS

- Write a comparison and contrast essay about one or more creation myths.

- Evaluate the tender-minded versus tough-minded dialectic. Write about the arguments in favor of both viewpoints.

Creative Prompts

- Write, paint, draw, or compose your own creation myth.
- Write the script of a conversation between a tender-minded mythologist and a tough-minded mythologist.

NOTES

1 Campbell, *The Flight of the Wild Gander: Explorations in the Mythological Dimension*, quoted on 43.
2 Ibid, 44.
3 Ibid, 44.
4 Ibid, 45.
5 Ibid, 49.
6 Ibid, 50.
7 Ibid, 52.
8 Ibid, 52.
9 Ibid, 53.
10 Ibid, quoted on 53.
11 Ibid, quoted on 53.
12 Ibid, 53.
13 Ibid, 54.
14 Ibid, 55.

"For the bedrock of the science of folklore and myth is not in the wisps and strays of metaphor, but in the ideas to which the metaphors refer."

—THE FLIGHT OF THE WILD GANDER, *page 56*

Chapter IV

Mythogenesis

Chapter Summary

LEGEND OF THE SACRED PIPE

This chapter begins with the story of the Sacred Pipe, from the Oglala Sioux. In this myth, two Sioux braves see a beautiful woman wearing white buckskin while they are out hunting. The first brave is compelled by desire to approach her. When he does so, he is covered over by a cloud. After the cloud clears, all that remains of him is a pile of bones and a batch of writhing snakes. The second, more cautious brave follows the woman's instructions to return to the village in order to prepare a ceremonial lodge. The lodge has twenty-eight poles, one for every day of the month. The pole in the center represents the Great Spirit supporting the universe. Campbell points out that the lodge is a symbolic counterpart of the universe.

When the woman arrives at the lodge, she walks around the people gathered inside, going in a sunwise direction from east to south then west and north. She takes a pipe out of her bundle. The red stone bowl of the pipe represents the Earth, with a buffalo calf carved in the center, representing all the four-legged animals. The seven circles on the pipe indicate the seven rituals in which it will be used. The twelve feathers hanging from the stem are those of the Spotted Eagle. The stem is all that grows upon the earth. "When you smoke this pipe," she tells the assembled gathering, "all these things join you, everything in the universe: all send their voices to Wakan Tanka, the Great Spirit, your Grandfather and Father."[1] A ritual is performed and a prayer recited to identify all the pieces of the pipe with the bodies of the celebrants, after which the woman leaves the lodge, saying "in me there are four ages: and at the end I shall return."[2] She walks off towards the horizon, rolls over and turns into a young red and brown buffalo calf. She then goes farther, rolls over, and becomes a white buffalo. And finally she goes farther, rolls over, and becomes a black buffalo. She then bows to the four directions and disappears. The sacred woman personifies the feminine aspect of the cosmic buffalo.

This marvelous story was told by the great visionary seer Black Elk, Keeper of the Sacred Pipe, in 1947–48. The Oglala Sioux had migrated to the plains in 1680 or so from the forest lakes and marshes of the Upper Mississippian cultures.

Campbell compares this story with the Greek myth of Actaeon, who saw the goddess Artemis bathing in the woods. Artemis turns Actaeon into a stag and his own hounds hunt him down and devour him. Campbell also notes the similarity of the sacred lodge to a temple. He wonders rhetorically if we should ignore shared mythic motifs like these, according to the focus in academia on the importance of cultural differences and particularities.

Instead, he asks us to "look further, with an uncommitted eye, and try to judge for ourselves,"[3] offering several key points regarding a comparative mythological approach to the Legend of the Pipe:

- There are twenty-seven supports of the lodge plus the central pole, so twenty-eight supports of the universe.
- The snakes that devour the first brave represent his passions (like Actaeon).

"The great caves were not domestic sites but sanctuaries of the men's rites: rituals of the hunt, of generations living by the hunt, and of initiation to the mythological substratum of their rigorous lives."

—THE FLIGHT OF THE WILD GANDER, *page 76*

- 27 = 3 x 3 x 3 (one of Campbell's favorite Goddess numbers).

- Campbell cites Jung on the numbers 3 (which represents time) and 4 (which represents space), which together represent the field of all phenomenal forms analogous to Immanuel Kant's *a priori* structures of the mind.

- The buffalo's twenty-eight ribs are the counterpart of the monthly cycle of the moon. Both return every month, "miraculously renewed, like the Moon Bull of the archaic Near East, the animal vehicle of Osiris, Tammuz, and, in India, Śiva."[4]

- Campbell refers to the Biblical moon god Sin, after whom Mount Sinai was named, and in whose honor Aaron was conducting the festival of the Golden Calf when Moses returned, his face shining with horns of light, like the moon.

Campbell also notes key comparisons with the mythologies of the ancient world, connecting the "Sacrificial Lamb, the Sacrificial Bull, and the Cosmic Buffalo."[5] He observes that Black Elk could have been interpreting those symbols as well when he said that the buffalo represents both the universe and the field of time, "dying yet ever renewed," and the eternal Great Spirit, "the center that is everywhere and around which all revolves."[6]

Campbell also connects the ritual purification of the sacred pipe with Vedic rituals in India, "where the altar and every implement of the sacrifice is identified allegorically with both the universe and the sacrificing individual: 'He who is in the fire, he who is here in the heart, and he who is yonder in the sun: he is one.'"[7]

"We have to accept the fact that the walls have lately been knocked from around all mythologies—every single one of them—by the findings and works of modern scientific discovery."

—THE FLIGHT OF THE WILD GANDER, *page 81*

Chapter IV: Mythogenesis

But where did the myth of the White Buffalo Woman come from? What was her mythogensis? As Campbell suggests, "let's follow her to her source"[8] in the following sections of this essay.

THE NEOLITHIC BACKGROUND

This section focuses on the archaic roots of the symbolism of the sacred "sunwise" turn, the cosmic ceremonial lodge, and the cycle of the four ages, all in the context of the planting cultures of the Neolithic period and their manifestations in the Americas. The Mississippian cultures along the Ohio and Missouri rivers show Mesoamerican influences from as early as 500 BCE ascending the Mississippi from Mexico. Evidence for the backgrounds of these early agricultural mythologies comes from the Tehuacán Valley caves (7200–2300 BCE), Tamaulipas (7000–2200 BCE), and Peruvian cultures (3800–3000 BCE), with possible trans-Pacific influences at Huaca Prieta in northern Peru (around 1016 BCE), and the presence of Japanese Jomon pottery in Ecuador (3000 BCE). These influences may have followed the west-to-east ocean currents from the Japanese island of Kyushu to Hawaii, to the Guayas coast of Ecuador (3190 BCE).

Campbell broadens the fields of comparison by noting the worldwide distribution of swastika and color symbolism, taking his lead from Leo Frobenius, who proposed movements from Africa to India, Southeast Asia, Oceania, and America. This line of speculation opens further possibilities of diffusion from China and Angkor Wat, as suggested by the mysteries of Mayan architecture and the sculptural artifacts of Chiapas, Tabasco, Campeche, and Peten, as far back as the Toltec period.

THE PALEOLITHIC BACKGROUND

The story of the White Buffalo Woman might include agricultural mythic influences from the far distant past, but it also shows unmistakable signs of a hunting culture. Hunting mythologies typically tell of a covenant or agreement between the people and the animals that they hunt.

Campbell suggests that the symbolic lore of the North American buffalo hunt originates in Paleolithic culture, even earlier than Neolithic farming villages. As evidence he cites Clovis Point spearheads from 35,000 BCE; artifacts of the Mojave Desert, north of Barstow, dating back to 40,000 BCE; and the Folsom Point spearhead from 8,000 BCE. He emphasizes parallels to the Paleolithic caves in Southern France and Northern Spain (such as Altamira, Lascaux, and Trois-Frères). One finds in those caves handprints with finger joints missing—suggestive details, given that the plains people of the Buffalo Hunt also chopped off fingers as offerings to the sun, or *Wakan Tanka*. Archetypal images of the European Paleolithic period include the iconic "sorcerer" of the Trois-Frères cave (depicted with stag antlers, a beard, the paws of a lion, the tail of a horse, and the legs of a man), and the "shaman" of Lascaux (lying in a trance, wearing a masked costume, and holding a staff with a bird head beside a bison) dating from 20,000–11,000 BCE. Campbell concludes that we have followed White Buffalo Woman to her source in the vast area of the Paleolithic Great Hunt, from the Pyrenees, to Lake Baikal in Siberia, Asia, across the Bering Strait, down the Mississippi.

Following this line of reasoning, the mythogenetic zone of the original mythologies of the Paleolithic hunting cultures was

Chapter IV: Mythogenesis

the Old World, while the Americas represent zones of diffusion, during periods of migration across the Bering Strait and southwards into North America. At this time the landscape was mythologized by the process of what Campbell calls "land-taking," which involves the spiritual assimilation of the newly entered territory into a myth "already carried in the immigrant's heart."[9] In addition, in the process of acculturation, one culture absorbs elements of another culture after an encounter.

Both the Sioux and the Pawnee, therefore, combined the great Buffalo of the Paleolithic with the Mexican myth of four world ages. This image of four ages appears also in India's tradition of the four ages called *yugas* (in which the cow of virtue loses a leg at the end of each).

Or are these similarities between cultures less a process of diffusion than of convergence, in which similar myths arise independently? Sir James George Frazer speculated that the similarities among all humans could give rise to similar mythic images. This problem is further complicated by Jung's theories about the archetypes of the collective unconscious.

THE PSYCHOLOGICAL BASE

In this section, Campbell uses the term "psychological" to refer to the imprinting of social ideas from infancy onwards. Social conditioning varies widely from culture to culture, and no single image has been found to be universally innate to the psyche. Furthermore, scientific discoveries have rendered practically all mythic images obsolete, from the point of view of understanding the universe. However, there are basic biological experiences that

practically all of us do share, such as the birth trauma, parents, excretory functions, sexuality, and relations to our peer groups.

In many societies, these developmental imprinted ideas are changed dramatically during rituals of initiation, such as those performed at puberty, which center on the death of infancy and rebirth into adulthood. These rituals often involve bodily mutilation (circumcision, clitoridectomy, tattooing, ritual defloration) to signify the transition from one stage of development to another. "Through these forceful rearrangements of the references of the father image, mother image, birth idea, etc.," Campbell suggests, "the reflex system of the whole psyche is decisively transformed."[10] In other words, the highly emotional and irreversible nature of these initiations bring about a profound change in the psyche, or psychology, of anyone who experiences them.

Mythology can support these changes. For example, a child might associate a Mother Goddess mostly with her own mother. But after undergoing a puberty ritual, the new young adult might be able to experience the Mother Goddess more cosmically, as "the life-producing, disciplining, and supporting aspect of the world,"[11] of which her own mother is just one example.

Mythologies do support an individual society's particular needs for shaping adult behavior, which are different from culture to culture and from time to time. But one common theme in all mythologies is to prepare us to face our own death, as well as the powerful mysteries of our own unique personalities such as love, hate, fear, disdain, wonder, terror, and joy.

THE PERSONAL FACTOR

Ultimately, Campbell points out, it is not social leaders but individual dreamers, like Black Elk and medicine men, who create—or rather, receive—the legends and myths that support the cultural order.

Black Elk's Great Vision ends with an epic journey, as the tribe follows four ascents along roads of four colors. During these climbs, a man painted red walks to the center of the gathered people, lies down and rolls, and when he gets up turns into a bison.

Many aspects of this vision—such as the tree at the center of the world, the crossroads, the world hoop, the world mountain, guides, world guardians—also appear in myths from other cultures. But here they appear in the unique particularities of the Oglala Sioux, delivered by a single individual: Black Elk. They represent one young boy's personal vision, foreshadowing his people's transition from hunting to agriculture, to extreme hardship and difficulty, and ultimately beyond.

Complementary Reading from Campbell's Work

For more about mythologies from hunting and agricultural societies, see *The Historical Atlas of World Mythology: Vol. I, The Way of the Animal Powers: Part 2, Mythologies of the Great Hunt* (Harper Collins, 1988) and *The Historical Atlas of World Mythology: Vol. II, The Way of the Seeded Earth: Part 3, Mythologies of the Primitive Planters: The Middle and Southern Americas* (Harper Collins, 1989).

"Mythology and the rites through which it is rendered open the mind ... not only to the local social order but also to the mystery dimension of being—of nature—which is within as well as without ..."

—THE FLIGHT OF THE WILD GANDER, *page 86*

For more of Campbell's work regarding goddess mythologies, see *Goddesses: Mysteries of the Feminine Divine*, edited by Safron Rossi in *The Collected Works of Joseph Campbell* (New World Publishing, 2013) and *In All Her Names*, edited by Joseph Campbell and Charles Musès (HarperSanFrancisco, 1991).

FURTHER READING

Eshleman, Clayton. *Juniper Fuse: Upper Paleolithic Imagination and the Construction of the Underworld*. Wesleyan, 2003.

Momaday, N. Scott. *The Way to Rainy Mountain*. University of New Mexico Press, 1976.

Neihardt, John. *Black Elk Speaks: The Complete Edition*. Bison Books, 2014.

DISCUSSION AND ESSAY QUESTIONS

- Choose an image from one of Campbell's books related to the Native American or Middle Eastern mythologies discussed in this chapter and offer some creative reflections and analysis, perhaps including some further reading on the subject of Paleolithic and Neolithic cultures.

- This chapter describes many sources of mythology: a single individual, our shared human psychology, the unique environments of particular cultures (or societies), and metaphysical mysteries beyond the day-to-day world. Describe what each of these sources can and cannot contribute to an individual myth.

Chapter IV: Mythogenesis

CREATIVE PROMPTS

- Describe a dream or experience in your life that you might consider visionary, i.e., a glimpse into another reality. Discuss its impact on your life. If you haven't had such a moment, create one by writing, painting, dancing, or composing.

- Does Black Elk's vision carry meaning for you personally? Write, paint, or compose music about what his dream tells you, and the most vivid images from it that capture your imagination.

NOTES

1 Campbell, *The Flight of the Wild Gander: Explorations in the Mythological Dimension*, 63.
2 Ibid, 66.
3 Ibid, 61.
4 Ibid, 62.
5 Ibid, 62.
6 Ibid, 62.
7 Ibid, 64.
8 Ibid, 67.
9 Ibid, 79.
10 Ibid, 84.
11 Ibid, 84.

Chapter V
The Symbol Without Meaning

Chapter Summary

This chapter is the richest and longest of the book, full of insightful reflections on key themes central to Campbell's thinking about mythology and providing an extraordinary overview of the cultural foundations of myth in the Ancient World.

PART I

THE IMPACT OF MODERN SCIENCE

Paradigm shifts in science over the last few centuries have generated a "new image of the universe,"[1] so that the old, mythological cosmologies can no longer be taken literally. For example, according to the principles of contemporary physics, if she were traveling at the speed of light during the Assumption, the Virgin Mary would not even be out of the Milky Way galaxy yet! This goes far beyond the shift from a geocentric to a heliocentric paradigm of the sixteenth and seventeenth centuries, and the basic principles of Newtonian physics. After Einstein's work on relativity, and breakthroughs in astronomy that rapidly followed, leading thinkers began to develop symbolic interpretations of the old mythologies—which could no longer be taken literally as descriptive paradigms of the cosmos—but we still need to create new myths in their place.

These insights lead Campbell to a discussion of the symbolic functions of science itself: metaphysical propositions, he

"*The phantasmagoria of dream and vision are of 'subtle matter.' Extremely fluent and mercurial, they are not illuminated, like gross objects, from without, but are self-luminous.*"

—THE FLIGHT OF THE WILD GANDER, *page 100*

Chapter V: The Symbol Without Meaning

suggests, following Rudolf Carnap (1891–1970), are like music or lyric poems, and function as metaphors representing the ultimately unknowable mysteries of the cosmos. What, then, is the nature of metaphor and symbol? To answer this question, Campbell evokes C.G. Jung's distinction between a sign and a symbol: the former clearly stands for something in the known world, while the latter points beyond itself to an unknown dimension of meaning. (Jung uses the moon as such a symbol, since one side sheds light on the known world, and the other points into the darkness of the cosmos.)

Developing this difference between signs and symbols, Campbell introduces the Hindu distinction between *pratyakṣa*, referring to that which is perceptible to the senses, and *parokṣa*, referring to that which is beyond the eye, similar to Platonic ideas which are "purely intelligible, spiritual."[2] A living mythology unites both of these into a single, cohesive order.

THE MYTHIC FORMS OF ARCHAIC CIVILIZATION

This section of the chapter provides a detailed overview of the emergence of the cultures of the ancient Near East. Campbell regards this area as a mythogenetic zone, meaning a place that gave rise to myths. He focuses on the contrast between earlier Paleolithic cultures of the Great Hunt and the more recent agricultural cultures that developed into the first cities along the Tigris-Euphrates rivers.

There were psychological and social tensions in the shift from the hunter to the farmer, and from the independent individual to the individual as a small part of a larger society, contained in and dependent on the village. During this period the goddess images of the Paleolithic hunt developed into the Neolithic "mother-goddess"[3] figurines found in places like the city of Çatal Hüyük in Anatolian Turkey.

In addition, the earliest association of swastika and mandala symbolism is found in carved mammoth ivory from a late Paleolithic site near Kiev. This association of the swastika and the mandala would be important in Neolithic cultures of Samarra in Iraq and Halaf in Syria and Turkey. Later, Halafian symbology of the bull, the goddess, the dove, and the double ax—already present "two thousand years before in the chapels of Çatal Hüyük"—will become the prototypes of the Minoan mythologies of ancient Crete, and then find their "culmination in the great historical religions of Ishtar and Tammuz, Isis and Osiris, Venus and Adonis, Mary and Jesus."[4]

Campbell offers this useful and detailed classification of the emergence of agriculture and the cities in the ancient Near East:

- Stage 1: Proto-Neolithic, from 9000 BCE. Natufian. Artifacts found in Mt. Carmel Caves in Palestine; Helwan, Egypt; Beirut and Yabrud; Kurdish Hills, Iraq. Evidence suggests nomadic hunting tribes who supplemented their diet by gathering some early grains.
- Stage 2: Basal-Neolithic, from 7500–4500 BCE. Village farming appears.
  - Substage 1: Aceramic Neolithic from 7500 BCE. Jericho in Palestine. Brick houses emerge, a stone wall around the village and a stone watchtower. Worship of human skulls and ancestors.

- Substage 2: Ceramic Neolithic from 6500 BCE. Çatal Hüyük, Turkey. Pottery emerges, wall painting, shrines, mother goddess figurines, and sacred bucrania (or bull skulls).
- Substage 3: Early Chalcolithic from 5500 BCE. Early metalwork emerges and increasingly beautiful pottery.

• Stage 3: High Neolithic (also known as Middle and Late Chalcolithic), 4500–3500 BCE. Intricate geometric ceramics of Halaf, Samarra, and Obeid. Villages with carpentry and house building, agriculture and domestic animals, specialized social roles and priestly orders.

Regarding the development of geometric motifs in the ceramics of the High Neolithic, Campbell asks a crucial question: Do these geometrical mandalas represent inborn, universal structures of the psyche (as Jung would have it), or do they represent a "certain phase of social development" associated with villages and cities?[5] Or do they combine those two influences, the psyche impacting art forms and the social order, and the social order effecting a fundamental restructuring of the psyche? It is a question—sincerely posed and not definitively answered—that later critics of Campbell's inclination towards Jung and universalist theories of myth would, for the most part, ignore.

THE NEOLITHIC-PALEOLITHIC CONTRAST

Campbell observes that Neolithic hunting cultures probably required less specialized work than Paleolithic agricultural people did. In a hunting culture, each adult possessed mostly the same knowledge and abilities as everyone else. That meant that

"Mythological cosmologies, it now must be recognized, do not correspond to the world of gross facts but are functions of dream and vision ..."

—THE FLIGHT OF THE WILD GANDER, page 101

everyone could think of themselves as a complete person, able to survive alone or with the group.

In farming cultures, people had to specialize their work, finding a narrower niche that would make a valuable contribution to society but probably wouldn't allow them to survive on their own.

Campbell theorizes that this shift from self-sufficiency to dependence on society was stressful, and gave rise to new mythological stories and images to help people cope. For example, the mandala could have offered farming people an image of wholeness to help them feel more complete. He suggests that the new myths that emerged formed the foundation for later myths, such as Ishtar and Tammuz, Isis and Osiris, Venus and Adonis, and Mary and Jesus. He also wonders what new mythological images we might need as we continue the rapid shift out of farming culture and into a more technology-based way of life.

- Stage 4: The Hieratic City State (3500–2500 BCE). First Sumerian cities of the Tigris-Euphrates delta (Ur, Kish, Lagash, Eridu, Sippur, Shuruppak, Nippur, and Erech).
    - Ziggurats with chapel on top for ritual union of Queen as Goddess, and King as God.
    - Walled city organized as a mandala, with the central sanctum of the palace and ziggurat. Mathematical calendar to regulate the city's rituals with the passages of the sun, moon, and stars (Venus).

- Writing, decimal number system used for business transactions, sexagesimal (based on the number 60) number systems for ritual space and time: 360 degrees in a circle, 360 days of the year +5 for days of feast and festival. The days of the year correspond to a spatial mandala, where the fifth point indicates the place where eternity enters time.

- City culture spreads to Egypt (2800 BCE), Indus Valley (2600 BCE), China (1500 BCE); Peru and Mesoamerica (1000 BCE, via the Pacific?).

These first cities were an imitation of the celestial order, a "middle cosmos or mesocosm, between the macrocosm of the universe and the microcosm of the individual."[6] People believed that their destiny was intertwined with the organism of the universe, modeled on the observable celestial order of the planets, the stars, and the constellations. This paradigm brings the individual into an orderly relationship to society, and with a higher power at work in the cosmos, similar to the Platonic Intellect, the idea of *ma'at* in Egypt, *dharma* in India, *tao* in China, and, I would add, the concept of *logos* in Heraclitus and the Gospel of John.

In this context, myths and rituals bring the microcosmos of the individual person into alignment with the macrocosmos of the universe, by way of the mesocosmos of the culture.

Chapter V: The Symbol Without Meaning

PROBLEM OF THE NEW SYMBOL EMERGENT

As Campbell has pointed out before, the human psyche is not inborn, but is in some sense imposed on each of us beginning when we are born and as we mature. Therefore, none of us is truly whole. Each of us is imprinted with only a part of what we could have been.

When mandalas first appeared, the image in their center represented a higher power, often in the form of a deity. Since the Renaissance, however, the individual soul occupies the center. Campbell wonders if we can view the mandala not only as a simple sign (as he discussed at the beginning of this chapter), but also as a mysterious symbol, pointing beyond itself to the ultimate source of all.

PART II

THE SHAMAN AND THE PRIEST

This section develops a dialectic that recurs throughout Campbell's teaching and writing. He suggests that indigenous hunters of the American Great Plains (such as the Sioux)—who inherited the lifestyle and mythologies of pre-historic Paleolithic cultures—focus their religious life on the individual. Through fasting and vision quests, this individual receives guiding visions. Planting tribes, on the other hand, such as the Hopi and Zuni pueblos, organize life around ceremonies of "Masked Gods,"[7] the Kachinas. Similarly, the shaman of the hunting cultures gains power after experiencing a "personal psychological crisis"[8] which brings him or her in contact with unique spiritual visitors. By contrast, the priest of the planters is ceremonially initiated into a social order, or "a recognized religious organization,"⁹ serving gods known to the entire village.

Campbell illustrates the dialectic between the shaman and the priest with the origin legend of the Jicarilla Apache in New Mexico. In this myth, the gods (called Hactcin) create the world, and then an eclipse follows. The shamans fail to bring the sun back, and the animals collect food but fail as well. So the Hactcin summon Thunder Beings of four colors to create sand paintings with seeds planted in each of the four sacred mountains, which merge to become a single mountain that rises upwards. The Hactcin then select twelve shamans and six clowns to perform a dance that will make the mountain grow. Four ladders of light are then constructed so that the people can ascend from lower worlds to emerge on the earth, like children being born from their mother. And so, Campbell concludes, the shamans have been eclipsed and replaced by a priesthood.

THE WILD GANDER

In Campbell's view, the main purpose of mythologies in agricultural cultures is to suppress individualism and align the people with the needs of the collective. This section focuses on mythological figures who defy that social pressure and instead bring fire to a culture, such as Prometheus, Raven, Coyote, and Jackal. Campbell calls them the "super shamans" or "trickster-heroes of the Paleolithic hunters."¹⁰ Their original prototypes are to be found among the Paleo-Mesolithic cultures of Siberia, at a place called Mal'ta, near Lake Baikal, where female figurines and carved flying geese were found, made from mammoth ivory.

Migrations across the Bering Strait, beginning as early as 40,000 BCE and continuing up to the first millennium CE, brought the mythologies of the Paleolithic hunters into the Americas from the north. So, Campbell argues, we can track a continuity of mythologies from the Pyrenees, to Lake Baikal, and on to the "final twilight"[11] of the buffalo hunt on the North American Plains of the Sioux.

Shared images of the shamanistic trance with the flight of a wild bird (gander, duck, eagle, woodpecker, raven, vulture) are found throughout this broad domain, the origins of which can be tracked back to the Paleolithic: the carved geese found at Mal'ta; the Lascaux cave painting of a shaman in trance, wearing a bird mask and holding a staff with bird on top, lying prone beside a bison; the bird costumes of Siberian shamans, who are conceived by their mothers via the descent of a bird. These bird symbols also survive as soul birds in the Egyptian Book of the Dead, and in the nomenclature of Hindu master yogis, who were called *haṃsas* and *paramahamsas*: "wild ganders" and "supreme wild ganders."[12]

MYTHOLOGIES OF ENGAGEMENT AND DISENGAGEMENT

Campbell suggests that religious symbols have two functions: first, engagement with society, and second, disengagement with the world in order to experience states of ecstatic transcendence.

Furthermore, Campbell identifies two kinds of the unknown: the "relatively unknown" and the "absolutely unknowable"[13] Symbols of the relatively unknown include imagery from the unconscious which appears in the dreams and visions of saints and other holy people, as well as mythological history and

"The myths and rites constellate a mesocosm—a mediating, middle cosmos, through which the microcosm of the individual is brought into relation to the macrocosm of the universe."

—THE FLIGHT OF THE WILD GANDER, *page 123*

Chapter V: The Symbol Without Meaning

cosmology. The absolutely unknowable, however, is completely beyond knowing. Symbols can propel the soul closer to the absolutely unknowable by giving the soul something to release. In other words, the point of the symbol is to let it go.

As an example of relatively unknown symbols, Campbell relays the account of a Tungus shaman's illness, in which the young man saw visions of his ancestors. These symbols enabled the young man to engage with his society as a shaman.

THE FLIGHT BETWEEN TWO THOUGHTS

To illustrate a symbol of disengagement and the search for ultimate liberation, Campbell begins with the yoga traditions of the Indus River (2500–1500 BCE). This example also illustrates the mythological conflict between complex agricultural societies and individually oriented, shamanistic hunting cultures.

Campbell then charts four stages in the mythic transformation of shamanistic titans:

1. The shaman or titan seeks to use demon magic to overthrow the gods out of hubris, or pride.

2. The shaman or titan renounces or destroys earth and heaven—or everything symbolized by the mandala—but only for himself. Here Campbell pauses to define a symbol as something that evokes and directs energy. When we give a symbol meaning, we engage its energy to ourselves. When we withdraw meaning from it, the energy releases and we disengage from the world of the senses.

3. The shaman or titan looks upon the whole world without judgment and sees all things as expressions (or epiphanies) of "the One Holy Power."[14]

4. The shaman or titan realizes the paradoxical truth that we are both bound by our engagement in space and time, and we are also ultimately free, or disengaged. Because we are inherently free even as we experience our lives, there is nothing to escape.

Chanting the sacred syllable AUM is one way to reach this mysterious unknown, and so is the shaman's trance. This "seed" syllable was of particular interest to Campbell throughout his writing and teaching. In Sanskrit lettering, AUM is formed by the body of the dancing Shiva: A = waking consciousness; U = dream consciousness; M = deep sleep (mystical union of the knower and the known). The silence of the void is between and beyond all forms: "The world, the entire universe," Campbell concludes, "its god and all has become a symbol—signifying nothing: a symbol without meaning."[15] Hence the title of this remarkable chapter.

Campbell introduces the example of the Buddha's sermon in which he simply lifted a single flower. Only one monk, Kashyapa, apprehended the Buddha's message. Campbell suggests that Kashyapa's perception of the flower cleared so much that they left no room for concepts about the flower, opening the way for Kashyapa to experience enlightenment. Drugs, religion, art, dream, and other experiences can cause an experience of this sudden clarity of perception which Campbell calls a "sense of existence,"[16] or a feeling of being.

So symbols have two aspects: their sense (or feeling), and their meaning. Because mythological and religious symbols are no longer able to hold the social and physical meanings that they once did, Campbell suggests that we need more of the individual strength and self-reliance of people in pre-agricultural cultures. The work of individual wholeness, as described by C.G. Jung, involves disengagement, or dissolving our identification with society's symbols and instead finding what Campbell calls "the meaning that is no meaning."[17] True freedom lies in the infinite expanse beyond the symbol's surface meaning.

COMPLEMENTARY READING FROM CAMPBELL'S WORK

For more about the impact of science, see the first chapter of *The Inner Reaches of Outer Space*, "Cosmology and the Mythic Imagination."

For more about the syllable AUM and Shiva Nataraja, see *The Mythic Image*, pages 356–62.

FURTHER READING

Eliade, Mircea. *Shamanism: Archaic Techniques of Ecstasy*. Princeton UP, 2004.

Halifax, Joan. *Shamanic Voices: A Survey of Visionary Narratives*. Penguin Compass, 1994.

Weiss, Peg. *Kandinsky and Old Russia: An Ethnographic Exploration*. Syracuse UP, 1984.

Coomaraswamy, Ananda K. *The Dance of Shiva: Fourteen Essays.* Rupe Publications India, 2013.

Zimmer, Heinrich. *Myths and Symbols of Indian Art and Civilization.* Princeton UP, 2021.

Discussion and Essay Question

Visit or remember a city you have been to that impressed you. What aspects of the design and functioning of the city reflect its mythological origins in the cities of ancient Mesopotamia? What aspects of the city reflect new mythological influences?

Creative Prompts

- Create a mandala design combining geometrical symbols with letters and meaningful words.
- Design a civic park modeled around mythological themes and symbols.

NOTES

1 Campbell, *The Flight of the Wild Gander: Explorations in the Mythological Dimension*, 97.
2 Ibid, p. 100.
3 Ibid, 105.
4 Ibid, 118–19.
5 Ibid, 112.
6 Ibid, 120.

7 Ibid, 126.
8 Ibid, 126.
9 Ibid, 126.
10 Ibid, 132, 131.
11 Ibid, p. 133.
12 Ibid, 134.
13 Ibid, 136.
14 Ibid, 145.
15 Ibid, 143.
16 Ibid, 150.
17 Ibid, 154.

"In many lands the soul has been pictured as a bird, and birds commonly appear as spiritual messengers: angels are modified birds."

—THE FLIGHT OF THE WILD GANDER, *page 134*

Chapter VI
The Secularization of the Sacred

Chapter Summary

THE TREE IN THE GARDEN

Campbell explains that the title of this chapter means bringing religious feeling, such as awe and wonder, into the non-religious, or secular, parts of our lives, and by extension into our experience of the whole world. He offers examples of this approach to spirituality in Asia, such as Hinduism, Buddhism, and Taoism. In contrast, he sees a tendency in religions such as Christianity to separate the sacred and the secular.

RELIGIONS OF IDENTITY

The title of this section refers to a religious experience of one's own divinity, or identifying with our own sacred nature. Campbell calls this experience "mythic identification."[1] This approach is based on the belief in an ultimate reality that transcends, or goes beyond, any kind of thought or description or idea, but at the same time it somehow acts as the source or support of the entire universe, including ourselves. Our consciousness (not our ego) is our sacred nature that connects us with that ultimate source. Campbell cites several mythic texts and images that reflect this view.

For example, the image of the "Lord of the Tree of Life" (Sumer, c. 2500 BCE) shows a horned god seated with the moon above his head and a cup in his hand that holds an ambrosial drink

"As I understand the phrase 'the secularization of the sacred,' it suggests an opening of the sense of religious awe to some sphere of secular experience, or more marvelously, to the wonder of this whole world and oneself within it."

—THE FLIGHT OF THE WILD GANDER, *page 157*

of immortality. The "Garden of Immortality" (Babylonian, 1750–1550 BCE) depicts a dual goddess known as Gula-Bau (a prototype of Demeter and Persephone in the Eleusinian and Orphic Mysteries) dispensing the fruit of immortality. The seal Campbell calls "The Lord and Lady of the Tree" (Sumerian, c. 2500 BCE) shows a god and a goddess tending fruit on a tree, with a serpent nearby.

Many images from other traditions also focus on the realization of the divinity within, including Śiva in Hinduism, Siddhartha in Buddhism, mystery cults of the classical world, the Roman novel *The Golden Ass*, the Well of Wisdom in Germanic myth, and an ale of immortality in Celtic myth. In none of these scenes is there a Fall, as there is in Genesis, where the woman and the serpent (which sheds its skin to be reborn) are demonized, and the Tree of Immortality prohibited.

Campbell finds similar metaphors of the divinity within in the figure of Śiva dispensing *amṛita* (the drink of deathlessness), the Bodhi Tree, Orphic Tablets, and Apuleius's novel *The Golden Ass*, in which the initiate becomes divine and identifies with the god. In Norse myth, the Well of Wisdom is found at the foot of the Tree of Life. In Welsh and Irish mythology, the sea-god Manannan dispenses his ale of immortality.

RELIGIONS OF RELATIONSHIP

In Biblical traditions, on the other hand, Campbell's "mythic identification" is considered to be heresy. Instead, these traditions emphasize relationship with a God who exists outside of humankind and all creation. This relationship can only happen through a social group. In Judaism, the group is defined by heredity. In Christianity, the group is defined as a religious organization. Further, Christianity literalizes the crucifixion of Christ not as a psychological or spiritual symbol, but as a factual, historical event, in which one person placated an angry god. Campbell calls this view "mythic dissociation,"[2] because the sacred is separated from everything else. In terms of the chapter title, the sacred is not secularized. In a state of mythic dissociation, Campbell sees what he calls "social identification,"[3] or identifying the self with the social group or religion, rather than with the sacred source to which the religion's symbols point. In Campbell's view, religious symbols, structures, and authority figures must eventually be left behind in order to identify with and follow the guidance of the divinity that fills the universe.

THE EUROPEAN GRAFT

Campbell argues that during the High Middle Ages, in the twelfth and thirteenth centuries—when the great Gothic cathedrals were rising, the first universities were forming, and the vernacular literature of the Arthurian Romances was being written—the value of individual experience was challenging the "dictates of authority,"[4] whether those of the Church or of the State.

Campbell finds evidence of this development in the life and letters of Abelard and Heloise, the poetic songs of the French Troubadours and the German Minnesingers, Gottfried von Strassbourg's *Tristan*, and, above all, in Wolfram von Eschenbach's *Parzival*, "the unsurpassed Grail romance of the greatest poet of the Middle Ages."[5] In the same spirit, some

seven centuries later, James Joyce (1882–1941) would famously assert the independence of the poet in his identification with Lucifer's rebellious proclamation: *"Non serviam!"* ("I will not serve!"). These are Stephen's words, at the end of *The Portrait of the Artist as a Young Man,* when he leaves Ireland to pursue his vocation as a poet and sets off for Paris, in order to escape the "nets" of home, fatherland, church.

EROS, AGAPĒ, AMOR

This section focuses on a theme close to Campbell's heart: love. He is especially interested in ideas about love that emerged during the High Middle Ages in the poetry and songs of the Troubadors in Provence, in the Minnesingers or singers of love in Germany, and in the Arthurian Romances of the Grail. In his lectures, he would often differentiate between *eros* (erotic love, which he called "the zeal of the organs in attraction to each other"), *agapē* (brotherly love of one's neighbor, and enemy), and *amor* (the personal love celebrated in the Romances).

There is an element of impersonality in the first two kinds of love; but *amor* involves two people who are refined and transformed by their love without sacrificing their individuality. By way of example, Campbell cites Gottfried's *Tristan,* in which a special kind of mystical love (*minne*) opens a religious dimension for the lovers. It is both "heretical and dangerous," because it defies the dictates of both the Church and the social order, and it is celebrated in the forest, in an "ancient heathen chapel, the secret grotto of the goddess," where a "wondrous crystalline bed" replaces the "Christian altar."[6] This was a radical gesture of rebellion. Until this point passionate love was only allowed as a metaphor for spiritual love of the divine, for example in the Christian, Hindu, and Jewish traditions, where spiritual love transforms human *eros* into sacred *agapē*. In *amor*, on the other hand, two individuals experience themselves as one without losing their individuality. Gottfried's celebration of the love between Tristan and Isolde suggests a conflict between AMOR and ROMA (the Catholic Church), whose very spellings reverse each other.

Gottfried himself said that the cave in his *Tristan* was "designed and built for lovers by giants in pre-Christian times."[7] This suggests that Gottfried's conception of the love grotto was derived from Celtic traditions rooted in the "old megalithic, Bronze Age Goddess of Many Names."[8] Much more than the lifeless dust in the book Genesis, this earth Goddess was an animate, vital mother figure.

But if the Tristan legend focused on the tragic conflict between nature and society, the Grail legends healed that breach, offering "a renewal of the Waste Land of the Christian social order through a miracle of uncorrupted nature, the integrity of a noble, resolute heart,"[9] or what Campbell elsewhere referred to as "the noble heart." This healing of the wasteland became a major preoccupation of the Romances of the twelfth and thirteenth centuries, including:

- *Perceval, Li Contes del Graal* (*The Story of the Grail*) (1181–91) by Chrétien de Troyes, in which the Grail is a dish studded with gemstones.

- *La Queste del Saint Graal (The Quest of the Holy Grail)* (1215–30), by an anonymous Cistercian monk, in which the Grail is the chalice of the Last Supper and its hero the saintly Galahad.

- Above all, Wolfram von Eschenbach's *Parzival* (c. 1215), which connects the Grail with its early Celtic and classical influences—an "ambrosial drink of the Celtic sea-god Manannan," and "the sacramental bowls of the late Classical Orphic sects"[10] such as the Pietroasa Bowl—while making the image relevant for Wolfram's own time.

Wolfram's Grail is neither a chalice nor a dish but a stone called "The Wish of Paradise" and "lapsit exillis" from the Latin *lapis exilis* which means "little, feeble, or uncomely stone."[11] This is also the name of the Philosopher's Stone in the *Rosarium philosophorum*, so that we must add alchemical imagery to the rich synthesis of mythologies in the Grail legends. Furthermore, Wolfram's stone is brought down from heaven by neutral angels, similar to the Islamic Ka'aba, in an effort to combine Islamic and Christian themes.

Wolfram's Grail is therefore a "talisman of cross-cultural associations"[12] that indicated humankind's release from the authority of the Church, perfected in individuality, and serving the world through love. For example, the Grail is found in a castle, not a church. Its guardian is a king, not a priest. It is carried by twenty-five young women, not by male acolytes. And Parzival restores the Waste Land through "the integrity of character, in the service of a singly focused love, *amor*."[13] It is true that the baptism of Feirefiz (Parzival's half-brother, a Muslim) at the end

"For we are all, in every particle of our being, precipitations of consciousness; as are, likewise, the animals and plants, metals cleaving to a magnet and waters tiding to the moon."

—THE FLIGHT OF THE WILD GANDER, *page 161*

of the poem is in the form of an ecclesiastical rite. But the baptismal font fills with water from the Grail stone, suggesting the "*aqua permanens*, the water of life of the alchemists and of the ancient pre-Christian world."[14]

Campbell concludes his analysis with three important points:

- In these twelfth- and thirteenth-century works a profound secularization of the sacred emerges, with love as the revealing and transforming power.

- In rejecting the authority of the Church, the poets drew on a pre-Christian tradition which recognized the divine in nature.

- The individual succeeds separately from the group, so that the hero must not follow the paths of others, but must instead discover his own. Each must enter the forest alone, where it is "most dark," with "no way or path."[15]

THE WESTERN INDIVIDUAL

For Campbell, the "wealth and glory of the Western world" comes from its respect for the individual.[16] Hence, the "Western Individual" is seen as "an end and value in himself, unique in his *im*perfection, in his process of becoming not what he 'ought' to be, but what he is, actually and potentially."[17] Campbell sees early roots of this view in ancient Greece, but believes that the arrival of Christianity in Europe placed the group before the individual. This was accomplished by concretizing mythology, or treating myth as historical fact. Campbell closes by suggesting that the Church "dehistoricize their mythology"[18] and

"Mythologized, the Cross of Christ was equated early in the Middle Ages with the Tree of Immortal Life, the tree forbidden in the Garden, and Christ crucified was its fruit; his blood, the ambrosial drink."

—THE FLIGHT OF THE WILD GANDER, *page 166*

instead look to science and historians for historical facts, and look to scripture for spiritual and psychological metaphor.

COMPLEMENTARY READING FROM CAMPBELL'S WORK

For more on these seminal ideas of Campbell's, see *The Masks of God: Occidental Mythology* (Penguin, 1991), *The Masks of God: Creative Mythology* (Penguin, 1991), and *The Romance of the Grail*, edited by Evans Lansing Smith in *The Collected Works of Joseph Campbell* (New World Publishing, 2015).

FURTHER READING

De Troyes, Chrétien. *Arthurian Romances*, Trans. William Kilber. Penguin, 1991.

Von Eschenbach, Wolfram. *Parzival*, Trans. A.T. Hatto. Penguin, 1980.

Von Strassbourg, Gottfried. *Tristan*, Trans. A.T. Hatto. Penguin Classics, 1960.

White, T.H. *The Once and Future King*. Ace, 1997.

DISCUSSION AND ESSAY QUESTIONS

- Choose an episode from the reading selections above for reflective analysis and commentary: What about the story captured your imagination?

- Watch a movie based on Arthurian Mythology and write an essay about how it handles the stories. Among the possible choices would be Eric Rohmer's *Perceval*, Hans Jürgen Syberberg's *Parzival*, John Boorman's *Excalibur*, Monty Python's *Holy Grail*, or *The Fisher King*.

CREATIVE PROMPTS

- Write, paint, or compose your own version of one of the Grail Romances.

- Write, paint, or compose a version of one of the Grail Romances from the point of view of a minor character in the story.

NOTES

1 Campbell, *The Flight of the Wild Gander: Explorations in the Mythological Dimension*, 160.
2 Ibid, 167.
3 Ibid, 168.
4 Ibid, 171.
5 Ibid, 171.
6 Ibid, 174.
7 Ibid, 179.
8 Ibid, 178.
9 Ibid, 179.
10 Ibid, 179.
11 Ibid, 180.
12 Ibid, 180.

13 Ibid, 180.
14 Ibid, 182.
15 Ibid, 183.
16 Ibid, 183.
17 Ibid, 183.
18 Ibid, 185.

"In these twelfth- and thirteenth-century works ... these lovers and poets returned consciously and conscientiously to an earlier, pre-Christian, native European order of conscience, wherein the immanence of divinity was recognized in nature and its productions ..."

—THE FLIGHT OF THE WILD GANDER, page 182-83

Final Thoughts from Evans Lansing Smith, PhD

It has been said that deep within our psyche and embedded in every cell we contain the whole history of our evolutionary development, stretching back through the layers of our biographical and ancestral lineage across the generations all the way back through the evolution of our species, itself emerging from the incomprehensible abyss of the creation of life on our immensely ancient planet, which miraculously appeared along with our solar system and galaxy born at some incalculable moment of cosmic creation.

It is also said that—under certain circumstances—we have direct access to this information, which, as Carl Sagan (1934–96) liked to point out, is encoded in the carbon of our fingernails, residue of the of the Big Bang. For some of us, this can happen during exalted states of non-ordinary consciousness, whether induced by deep states of dream and meditation, by near-death visions, or by any variety of religious ceremonies and initiation rites.

For me this deep reservoir of spiritual wisdom can be accessed by more ordinary means—that is to say, by reading. You might start by reading Campbell's wonderful books like *The Flight of the Wild Gander*, which, as we have seen, takes its readers on a magical tour through the course of human history and cultural development. Having provided the itinerary for the journey, I invite you now to undertake it on your own, set keel to breakers, and go forth on the godly sea.

About Joseph Campbell

Joseph Campbell was an American author and teacher best known for his work in the field of comparative mythology. He was born in New York City in 1904, and from early childhood he became interested in mythology. He loved to read books about Indigenous American cultures, and frequently visited the American Museum of Natural History in New York, where he was fascinated by the museum's collection of totem poles. Campbell was educated at Columbia University, where he specialized in medieval literature, and, after earning a master's degree, continued his studies at universities in Paris and Munich. While abroad he was influenced by the art of Pablo Picasso and Henri Matisse, the novels of James Joyce and Thomas Mann, and the psychological studies of Sigmund Freud and Carl Jung. These encounters led to Campbell's theory that all myths and epics are linked in the human psyche, and that they are cultural manifestations of the need to explain social, cosmological, and spiritual realities.

After a period in California, where he encountered John Steinbeck and the biologist Ed Ricketts, Campbell taught at the Canterbury School, and then, in 1934, joined the literature department at Sarah Lawrence College, a post he retained for many years. During the 1940s and '50s, he helped Swami Nikhilananda to translate the Upaniṣads and *The Gospel of Sri Ramakrishna*. He also edited works by the German scholar Heinrich Zimmer on Indian art, myths, and philosophy. In 1944, with Henry Morton Robinson, Campbell published *A Skeleton Key to Finnegans Wake*. His first original work, *The Hero with a Thousand Faces*, came out in 1949 and was immediately well received; in time, it became acclaimed as a classic. In this study of the "myth of the hero," Campbell asserted that there is a single pattern of heroic journey and that all cultures share this essential pattern in their various heroic myths. In his book he also outlined the basic conditions, stages, and results of the archetypal hero's journey.

Joseph Campbell died in 1987. In 1988, a series of television interviews with Bill Moyers, *The Power of Myth*, introduced Campbell's views to millions of people.

About the Author

Evans Lansing Smith, PhD, is core faculty in the Mythological Studies program at the Pacifica Graduate Institute in Santa Barbara, CA. He has taught at colleges in Switzerland, Maryland, Texas, and California. He is the recipient of awards for distinguished teaching and publication from Midwestern State University in Texas and the Pacifica Graduate Institute in California, and he was nominated for the International Writer of the Year by the International Biography Centre in Cambridge, England.

In the 1970s, Dr. Smith traveled with Joseph Campbell on mythological study tours of northern France, Egypt, and Kenya. His edited volume of Joseph Campbell's writings and lectures on the grail romances was published in 2015, and his edition of the *Selected Correspondence of Joseph Campbell* in 2019. He has also led mythological study tours focusing on the grail romances in England and France.

Dr. Smith's PhD in literature is from the Claremont Graduate School. He holds an MA in creative writing from Antioch International (London and Dublin), and a BA in English from Williams College. He is the author of a novel and two books of poetry, plus eleven books and numerous articles on comparative literature and mythology.

About the Joseph Campbell Foundation

The Joseph Campbell Foundation invites you to experience the power of myth. Building on the work of Joseph Campbell, we offer resources and community for those who hear the call to adventure.

For more information about Joseph Campbell and the Joseph Campbell Foundation, contact:

Joseph Campbell Foundation

www.jcf.org

www.ingramcontent.com/pod-product-compliance
Lightning Source LLC
Chambersburg PA
CBHW061809070526
44586CB00024B/2771